THE REVIEW MIRROR

David M. Harris

2013 Unsolicited Press Trade Paperback Edition
Copyright © 2013 David M. Harris
All Rights Reserved.
Published in the United States by Unsolicited Press.

ISBN:0615852602
ISBN-13:9780615852607

for Judy, of course

Table of Contents

The Review Mirror
Ex-patriot
Bed, 3 A.M.
Dal Segno
Ever After
Still Life
Right Fielder
Stranger
Nightfall
The Home for Aged Dogs
Toby
Burying the Cat
Rattle and Squeak and Moan
Knocked Incautious
Starting From a Line by Monica Mayper
Adrift
Wishes
Lost and Found
Hinda and the Leonids
The Possibility of Grace
Revelation
Pre-Madonna
Ecce Homo
Hineni
The Spear of the Moment
Poetry Cops
Why I am Not a Bear
Smoke and Rumble
Gyres
Shaping the Terrain
The Office of Breakfast
Memorial, London
October 1979
Fallen
In the Event of my Death
Acknowledgements

Poems

The Review Mirror

Rarely, soapy-handed, I stop
and look. Who is that?
I've seen that face
 in pictures,
 younger
smiling, hair dark and glossy.
Wrinkles covered
       by beard and bifocals, I might pass
       for fifty.

In pictures from my first wedding,
just a decade and a half ago, just yesterday.
       Slimmer, touched with gray,
without glasses.
       At my sister's seder
       the day before yesterday
       trim, with a head
full of grand, grandiose dreams.
       Where are the dreams?
       Smaller visions seep into their emptied space.
       Play center field for the Yankees? Cancel that.
       Make a family? Enter a check mark.
       Tear up the Pulitzer acceptance speech.
       Write a poem?
             Add up the score.
Subtract the losses.
Rinse off the past.
Start the new day.

Ex-patriot

Half a century ago, I carried a flag and grinned,
with the Young Republicans,
in my town's parade,
marching for a future
we could smell just past the horizon.

In 1970, we paused from marching and plotting
the perfect world to follow
Apollo's fires. Even later, at Canaveral,
standing by the great supine rocket,
I was moved from faction to remember
an explosion in space, a moment
of common fears and dreams.

Today, I watch the marchers,
fighting two more Asian wars,
try to puzzle out their chants and signs,
wave to them, and return to my magazine,
exhausted by hope.

Bed, 3 A.M.

Dog stretches out on one side,
a large, warm pillow.
Wife turns over, asleep,
tucks an arm around me.
Cat pounces,
then settles, blanketing my chest.
I lie still,
immobilized by love.

Dal Segno

Birds abound along the river.
I know the vireo by song if not by sight.
I recognize the robin, jay, and mourning dove,
not many more. I can tell a sparrow, but not which kind.
My eyes on dog and path, my mind
on Victoria's England. Jake runs ahead,
chasing one more something, and an unhurried
shape moves its slow shoulders and rises
-- and this I know, from all the icons and images --
this eagle before me shrugs off the earth
and lifts into apprehending flight.
All pauses in that moment.
Measured beats and a caesura,
and then the other birds resume
their rounds as though
nothing has changed.

Ever After

How many appletinis has it been?
when Snowy (all the girls use nicknames here)
says abruptly, "There are times I miss those
little fuckers." "They were pigs," says Cindy,
too loud. "They never washed a dish or fork
before you got there." Ari, tipsy, sips
her vodka-and-Clamato. "Didn't they
run out?" There's still a lot that's pretty new
to her. "Naw." Snowy waves a hand. "They would
just order more. They have a diamond mine,
you know."
                Every now and then they gather,
in back, in some dark, trendy bar, apart,
and let their hair down. Too bad they can't ask
Rapunzel.
                "I know what you mean." Belle sighs.
"I love my husband, but I can't help it--
I miss the beast he was when we were courting."
Snowy nods. "The dwarfs were pigs, but they were
fun. They sang a lot, and well." Now Cindy sighs.
"We know. I think you've mentioned it before."

It always comes to this. It's Cindy first
this time. "I need," she says, "to go to school.
I'll specialize in family law." They know
her history, and nod in sympathy.
Sweet Ari, once agog for legs and fire
and human toys, makes up her mind. "Marine
biology. Less icky than human.
I need to take up scuba diving, too,"
she slurs. "I love that library," Belle says,
"but sometimes, on dark nights, I dream of Jean
Cocteau."
                They pay the tab, and hoist Snow White
onto her feet, and struggle out to find
the golden coaches all lined up for them,
to take them home, each to her promised life,
each to her bleak and seamless happy end.

Still Life

One broken flower pot,
Broken neatly, two clean pieces laid together.
It might have fallen apart just now, spontaneously,
Except things do not fall apart like that.
Not even things as fragile as a terra cotta pot.
One torn, discarded pair of leather work gloves.
The hands that once needed their protection
Need it no longer, or the gloves no longer serve.
One concrete planter.
The geranium is red--no, not red but fuchsia--
The pansies two shades, dark and light,
Of a purple that edges toward blue.

I learned to see colors from Kate.
She could see a color
Match it from memory.
This was important to her.

One large crack in the stone slab
on which everything else rested.

Right Fielder

Neat's-foot oil and leather
pounding ball into glove
wrapping glove around ball
marrying with a book strap
teaching ball and glove to belong together
binding the tools of summer
to their tasks
possibilities and prospects.
Binding myself to baseball.
In March, we are all dreamers.

Stranger

Observe the dog.
He turns and meets
your eyes, returns to gaze
into the invisible. Finished,
he rises with inhuman
grace, loping
out into his
ineffable world.

Nightfall

In the grass, crickets sing the heat.
Behind me, dogs crunch kibble.
Above, silent bats prowl,
dark ghosts fluttering and swooping
over roof and yard,
careening through the trees and feasting,
blue-collar fliers, sweeping the air.
They draw me up,
to the Great Dog, to the Hunter,
out of the blood
that draws the mosquitoes.

The Home for Aged Dogs

We live at the home
for aged dogs, with blind
Viola and the two
whose ages we do not know.
Absent now are all the dogs
we brought to this house,
and soon Viola, no longer
able to explore her world, our town,
and towns beyond. She lies, resigned,
under my desk, waiting for some final
burst of clarity and light. Until then,
she dogs me around the house. For her,
we cannot move the furniture.

Toby

Lying there, on his last day,
dreaming, perhaps, of rabbits
or the days he dodged the leash,
borrowed freedom for an hour.
Or of those three days in the new neighborhood
chasing squirrels and adventure
but glad to see me when I collected him
after he drifted onto a stranger's porch,
lost and tired and hungry.
His legs, in dreams still strong
and under his control,
speed him through the woods
scattering the turkeys
gaining on the deer--
I wake him, lift his head
and carry him off
to where I tell myself
he will dream forever.

Burying the Cat

A curve of cairns.
Bear, Alley Oop, Rosenkrantz, and Guildenstern.
Rosette, but she was a guinea pig.
Now, in the summer heat,
through the rock and clay,
a grave for Yoda.
Digging is hard.

My first night in Judy's house, Bear
crawled under the covers between us.
Two years later Yoda
inched out of hiding,
let me scratch his head.

Hot work. Another inch.
Lever the rocks. Cut the roots.
Trim the earth to fit the box.
Shovel deep to keep coyotes
from following.
Digging is hard.

Prescription food, antibiotics, fluid drips:
what can be done, Judy does
and knows that the end is loss.

Burying is easy.
Filling in the hole is hard.

Rattle and Squeak and Moan

Where? I search in the still air.
The trail winds through these well-known woods
away from roads, machines, and men.
Animals have fled my clumsy feet,
the quiet, useless clash of my coins.
Up? I crane to see
the tops of half-dead pines,
high limbs crashing in a wind
I cannot feel.
I walk in their lee and hear
their call, their admonition.
Listen, they say, to the invisible.
Watch the inaudible.
The imperceptible fills the world
and all you must pay
is attention.

Knocked Incautious

Cozy little hillside house, big enough for books
and dog and me, safely wedged
into the earth. An hour from the hospital
of my birth. Terra cognita. Happy,
I guess.

The earth opened with an email,
blew me up with words and dreams.
A thousand miles later, I landed,
beyond the map's edge,
struck by you.

Starting From a Line by Monica Mayper

Full moon tonight. Venus in the west.
I rest awake in hilltop hammock and interrogate
the sky. It replies in booming silence, slides
through wine-dark toward black.
The emerging stars carry no news.
Their words come from minutes or ages
gone, never quite catching up.
                              Eyes and ears and nose
tell only of memories, leaving us
stranded in the fluid past.
Skin and tongue are intimate with time,
with the unchanging present and the fixity
of love.

Adrift

William Powell pours gin,
urbane, suave, full
of contained violence,
shaking with vermouth.

We dreamed of Thirties style--
Nick and Nora, Parker and Benchley--
married in the Algonquin
bought a cocktail shaker.
The new culturati.
Stoli Pertsovka
rich and fiery
as we imagined ourselves.
You can't get that any more.

At the patio bar of Hotel la Mariposa,
overlooking the Pacific sunset,
someone says, "Iguana."
I take his word,
but I certainly don't know.
I have a job in New York.
Here in Costa Rica,
The crew drifts toward the bar;
the company covers the tab.

See Dickens about gin.
Poor sots stumble into gutters
for lack of a splash of vermouth and
an olive.
We walk a fine line
we urban sophisticates.
When we remember.

I sat in noisy, chic bars with
vodka martinis
met my first wife
in the shadow of the Empire State
remembered an iguana

The Charleses used small glasses,
etched curved bowls
we could never find.

Cold, smooth, and sharp
the memory drifts

Now I sit atop a hill in Tennessee
a skink skittering over my shoe
sweet tea in my jar,
and keep a sharp eye out
for signs of me.

Wishes

In the woods,
boy at his side, stick in one hand,
cigar in the other, he posed
for the picture I am taking.

He watched his good child marry a man
of whom he approved, whom she would
divorce three years later, after
the boy was born.

He wanted to be a family man,
a good father and loving husband.
He glared into a mirror, saw instead
himself, his father, and me.

He swung an axe,
pulled a saw, hefted the logs
onto the wagon I helped him pull home.

Lost and Found

A box of tie tacks and collar stays.
A Party card, a corporate Zippo, a shilling.
How many generations are here?
Connections crystallize and sublime
A combat ribbon and a clown nose.
Memories drift in my drawer:
my father's pipe collides with his father-in-law's watch
tangles with a chain and my old wedding ring;
my memories
snarl with my education.

A shelf fills up:
my father's tea basket,
this broad-nibbed Parker,
mugs and inkwells and old pocket knives.
Lifetimes of accumulation and learning,
discovering, striving.
Shelves' contents slip away
at yard sales or into the trash.

Amassed knowledge has the weight of air.
My father's hard-won erudition dispersed
with the books my mother sold,
but his legacy
lay elsewhere.

A small box of pictures:
He is in uniform, against anonymous backgrounds.
On the backs: *August 1944*
or visiting *MI-6* or just *Lausanne*.
Meaning gone with him.

Should I be busy with labels and explanations?
All those images of travel and life and lore,
All fading in my hands.

There's nothing
important in my own junk drawer.

Should I dump it all?
Jewelry I never wear.
The replacement nib
for a pen long vanished.
Old keys to forgotten locks
What will fall in here?
What will I lose?
What will my daughter find?

Hinda and the Leonids

Deep into sleeptime, I kept my promise,
wrapped her in blankets, and woke her
into the cool night. I stood, waiting for our irises
to bloom. And the sky revealed itself.
I turned my almost-too-heavy bundle
to the east, and pointed. But in the time it takes
to turn, meteors vanish. Look, point,
turn, never fast enough to see
the brilliant flash on the sky. When she had missed
enough for one night, she had me
carry her inside, too sleepy
for disappointment, to the warmth
of her room and guardian bears. Another year,
another swarm, with me -- or with some boy --
a candent slash across the belly of the dark.

The Possibility of Grace

I
My daughter's first dance class:
run and twirl, play ballerina,
learn the unfamiliar gestures.
Dreams inch toward true.
Miss Marcy beams.
She planned to be
la prima.
Now, sponsored by the
Parks Department,
she watches her students and
looks happy.

II
My mother told me, once,
the happiest day of her life
was when she gave up performance.
But she never stopped dancing.

Revelation

The last black snow seeps into the sewer.
Tables bloom on Bleecker Street.
A student notes a haze
of green on the trees below, changes
her mind: short aqua skirt and yellow scooped blouse,
unveiling her to the unfamiliar sun, dazzling
the memories of the old men.

Pre-Madonna

The future was a rose of Sharon.
Young and lovely, born to influence,
descended from kings, destined to marry
some prince, to honor his family and be
a prominent wife and mother. Young notables
lined up to court
the priest's niece. No hick carpenter
for Mary.
Then the angel came.

Ecce Homo

Schlepping their expectations across the unpromising
land like one of his father's roof beams,
this fish in the desert leads his company, his words
remembered and revered; never a chance
to sit around and shoot the breeze.

No one to confide his human fears.
If he looks at Mary--all the girls seem
to be called Mary--or talks to her alone
the men glower and sulk.

Sometimes he wishes he were an older god.
Who has a better claim to wine
than he? Old Bacchus and Silenus get
to lift a jar; all he gets to raise is Lazarus.

Just once he'd like to be a normal guy.
But even if he tells a dirty joke, he knows
they'll never write that down.

Hineni
for Stanley Weinberger
Here I stand, the cantor sobs.
One word touches me, the rest moving air
throbbing over sense, beyond my head,
it falls and rises.

He passes through the people gathered
for this one day. His audience is not there;
today he speaks only to God. At this moment
he stands alone before the flame.

His voice betrays his years, but faith
has perfect pitch, no tremolo
when he stands before God for his people, for us.
No matter what we believe. He believes for us.

After this prayer I will leave, my small
cup of atheistic faith warm for now,
filled by the voice with aspiration,
filled by the voice almost to belief.

He leads us beyond ourselves, tempting us
to atonement and righteousness,
sings to God for us and prays
for the small miracle of faith.

The Spear of the Moment

On the point of indeterminacy, quantum
universes split and twist, wait
for the cat to jump or die,
to see who will be born,
and who
not.

Poetry Cops

They come to the door
with badges. The tall one,
the ponytail
and the denim jacket,
Sandburg's face stitched on the back,
asks politely,
"Could you show us
your poetry?"
The other, shorter,
broader, more like Gertrude
Stein, snorts and sneers.
At the kitchen table
refusing coffee
they examine notebooks,
loose printouts. They
mutter and make notes.
Finally they look at me.
The good cop says, "Not too bad."
The tough one talks of faulty
rhymes, dysfunctional meter, inept
lineation, enjambment and caesura.
"We'll let you off with
a warning, but pay
more attention to your craft."
Shaken but relieved, I
promise to do better
and watch them ring
a neighbor's bell.

Why I am Not a Bear

Smashing through the woods,
parting trees and bestriding logs,
scooping up wineberries, blackberries,
whatever is ripe and irresistible,
swiveling to listen and sniff the air,
the hairy beast is seized by a sudden
swivet--a hawk's hurtle, a chipmunk's
flustered flight--and thinks,
"That could be a poem."

Smoke and Rumble

Marvin treats her well.
In his small room:
one chair, one dresser, one picture framed in pine, a single bed
mounted on the footboard: the Evinrude
Rarely, Marvin starts the engine,
listens with a doctor's ear,
revs her once
and shuts her down before the other guys complain.
He doesn't need the noise and smoke
to cruise the lake
of his memories.

Gyres

For the last hour of Tennessee,
the roadside stipples with white
dots and drifts of cotton. The land levels,
browns, and now, in Missouri, sprouts that first
uneasy shape. A dark funnel seeks
the sky, slow and bleary, passed by
unresponding drivers. Then another behind,
and more. Distant spirals burgeon
from the reaped land. The wind wheels,
smoke-aroma, and then I pass
between the blackened fields and see the flames
twist the smoke into columns
rising from an ancient order.

Shaping the Terrain

It surfaced, a humpback through my lawn,
rounded and lumpy table
on which nothing would sit comfortable.
Halfway up the hill of that yard,
the punctuation of rock.

Jim sweated and cursed the fence posts in,
wanted stone for landscaping.
"Take what you want," I said.
He eyed the boulder
judging weight and depth and
just what it would take.

I considered paint.
Green or blue? Patterns? Still a rock.
For Bernini it might have become
a life-sized crouching lion, but
for me it was always that rock.
I hiked the old gravel quarries and thought,
"With a big enough hammer . . ."
I planted vines by it.
They failed to thrive.
The rock persisted, stubbornly itself

It outlasted me on that land.
What force could move it?
What hole would it leave?

The Office of Breakfast

It's Saturday, my day for flour, a splash
of oil, vanilla, all in order, honey, one homegrown
egg, and milk until it looks right. I stir with a fork--
always a fork--and make tea while the skillet heats.
Baking powder and sometimes fruit come last.
Not too much milk, not too much
heat. Not too long in the skillet.
I pour batter, sip the tea, wait and flip,
wait and lift, into the oven and pour
another. I've learned control.
My daughter, under firm instruction,
slouches up the stairs to rouse her mother
with filial promises of tea and breakfast
I greet the family with jam and syrup.
This day begins in peace with everyone at table
sharing the grace of griddle cakes.

Memorial, London

A formations of suits marches through the city of monuments,
full of an unknown purpose.
A puzzled old draft dodger
watches them parade.
Tweeds and flannels, pin-striped worsteds.
Crisp orders march the phalanxes
to face a squat stone.
One stands erect, silent,
unashamed, weeping.
I cannot hear the black suit address them.
These unknown men, their
monument, their cause:
I join their quiet tears,
their public grief.

October 1979

1
Barges pass against the cold sky
above the roads on which I cycle,
from Rotterdam to Delft,
to Amsterdam and Beek, almost
silent but for my ticking odometer.
Each revolution marking space,
time, vector.

Each morning I pluck a new town
from the hostel guide and plan my route.
Mail goes only out.

2
The land bulges with sea-level canals.
Distant barges creep by above my head.
Then bridges fling me up and over
to land, ticking softly,
in the next great green bowl.

Last year, my father's heart coughed
to get his attention.
Next year, it will stop.
This month I coast the Low Countries.

3
Sturdy Dutch bicycles,
antiques built for the long haul,
toil toward the compact towns,
Lelystad and Leeuwarden,
Zutphen and Venlo.

I pass them all.
Baskets full of cheese and cabbage,
cargo bikes hauling hammers and chickens,
riders stare at my backpack,
my saddlebags,
my swift, light ten-speed.

Belgians dreaming of Eddie Merckx
will stare at the weight I carry,
my slow, heavy ten-speed.

Near Utrecht, Fodor tells me,
bored soldiers built Austerlitz,
a pyramid for Napoleon.
In the soft autumn rain,
I snap a picture of
the neat Dutch hill.

I glimpse the water at Arnhem,
take the bridge the Germans held in '44.
Ahead lies Maastricht, where
d'Artagnan died in battle. Beyond that
I will be in Belgium.

4
The map, folded in its handlebar case,
guides my ride. I track progress
by the odometer clicks,
by signs and landmarks,
sinking into the map as I cannot
into the territory.

Fodor and Michelin shape
the journey and bind me to the roads.
I have no schedule
and no time for detours.

My mind is full of love and battles.
In New York, Renee
reads my letters carefully
then throws them away.
I ship Delftware home, and wooden shoes,
but carry only undeveloped images.

My days slide past
dotted with apple cake and churches,
museums and postcards.

5
South and east, the land rises into Flanders.
The road carries me through a tidy
Dutch forest, toward the Maas.
Lost in knowing where I am,
I look across to shining water.
A man sits quietly, puffing a pipe,
smoke drifting astern,
and I glide up from behind,
pumping easily,
gaining, inch by inch, on the barge

I count my miles, new totals every night.
How far tomorrow? What can I see
if I get there before it closes?

The bargee looks up at me. A brown mass
at his feet resolves into an incurious mastiff.
One hand on the helm, the man waves a greeting
with his pipe. I have learned this much:
"Goede dag!" across the field and water.
He returns, "Bonjour!"

6
Barges carry slow freight,
know where they are going,
arrive when they arrive.

Soon enough, I will need to climb.
I pace the man and dog and barge.
The road diverges from the canal, we wave again,
and I pedal toward the hills to come.

Fallen

Honestly, I never liked the towers. The renderings
made me think of Ozymandias.
Even so, I thought they'd last
a hundred years. Longer than me, at least.
On the trails with the dog,
listening to a book in the woods.
Another hiker, packed for survival,
seeking high ground.
I ran to the car radio for confirming dead air.
The syllabus flew out the window that day
and the next. Students told of
brothers at the high school by the towers,
family who worked in the towers,
when they had last visited the towers.
One student vanished
into his Army Reserve unit.
Seven miles from Indian Point
and its reactors, my sky
grew nervous with patrolling fighters.
The Marines went to war.
And then . . .

I told my story.
High school students turned up safe.
Those who worked in the towers came home,
or didn't. My classes returned
to the syllabus, without the Reservist.
The air patrols stood down.
The leaves fell.

In the Event of my Death

You'll find all my papers in the
file cabinets. Give them to the flames. My will
is in the strongbox.

  My will was never strong enough
to discard some cards from women
you never met. You have heard some
of their names. Like that scarf you hate
(the one Kathy knitted back in college), the cards
carry memories. Old signatures and sentiments
fall away with me. Burn them
or not.

  Burn me. Give the ashes to
the tomatoes. Give the tomatoes to
our friends for remembrance.

  Remember me as long as you can,
one generation, two. Tell
my stories. Tell the one about
the raft in Costa Rica.

  Tell yourself this:
at my end, I remembered you.

Special Thanks

I have been in a number of workshops and poetry groups over the years, and have received much help from the members of those groups, on these poems and others. Even if I could remember all the names, there is not space here for all of them. You know who you are, and I thank you.

Some people did give me special help and encouragement, perhaps without realizing it, and some of it not directly connected with poetry: George Effinger, Tom Disch, Jane Yolen, Damon Knight, Ginny Welsch, Beau Hunter, Mary Jo Bang, Janice Fuller, Peter Balakian, Tom Lux, and Bruce Smith.

And, of course, this book would probably not exist, and would certainly not be as good, without the particular attention, interest, and help of the staff of Unsolicited Press.

The following poems have been published previously, some in slightly different forms:
"The Review Mirror" in *My Poem Rocks*.
"Ex-Patriot" in *My Poem Rocks*.
"Bed, 3 A. M." in *Heyday*.
"Ever After" in *Gargoyle*.
"Still Life" in *Mphasis*.
"Right Fielder" in *Slow Trains*.
"Stranger" in *The Sigurd Review*.
"Nightfall" in *Pirene's Fountain*.
"Home for Aged Dogs" in *Slow Trains*
"Toby" in *Shine Review*.
"Rattle and Squeak and Moan" in *Pirene's Fountain*.
"Knocked Incautious" in *My Poem Rocks*.
"Starting From a Line by Monica Mayper" in *The Pedestal*.
"Adrift" in *Grasslimb Journal*.
"Wishes" in *The Labletter*.
"Lost and Found" in *Assisi*
"Hinda and the Leonids" in *The Labletter*.
""Revelation" in *Slow Trains*.
"Pre-Madonna" in *Strong Verse*.
"Ecce Homo" in *Smashcake*.
"The Spear of the Moment" in *Bull Spec*.
"Poetry Cops" in *Slow Trains*.
"Why I am Not a Bear" in *Strong Verse*.
"Smoke and Rumble" in *Other Poetry*.
""October 1979" in *Labletter*.
"In the Event of My Death" in *Grasslimb Journal*.

About the Author

David M. Harris spent twenty-five years working in publishing in New York, then threw it all over to go to graduate school and become a teacher. He got an MFA in fiction, then threw it all over to write poetry. After living in and around New York City all his life, he threw it all over to move to Tennessee to get married. Now he has a wife and child, a varying number of dogs, cats, fish, and chickens, and a 1972 MGB roadster. Along the way, he picked up some work in film production and some credits as a writer: a published novel, two produced screenplays, a weekly column that ran for about a year and a half in the local daily newspaper, a few short stories, a collection of essays, and a few dozen poems published in places like *The Pedestal*, *Labletter*, *Pirene's Fountain*, and *Gargoyle*.

www.ingramcontent.com/pod-product-compliance
Lightning Source LLC
Chambersburg PA
CBHW021028090426
42738CB00007B/940